DESTINED TO DO DAMAGE

By: Louis Trammell II

Foreword by Pastor Kim A. Davis
Senior Pastor, Ebenezer Full Gospel Baptist Church

Destined to Do Damage
By: Louis Trammell II

Cover Design By: Anelda L. Ballard
Cover Photograph by: Monica Trammell

Logo Designs By: Andre M. Saunders/Leroy Grayson
Editor: September Summer
Assistant Editor: Anelda L. Ballard

© 2010 Louis Trammell II
ISBN 978-0-9843255-8-0
ISBN 0-9843255-8-1
Library of Congress Control Number: 2010930952

All rights reserved. This book is protected under the copyright laws of the United States of America. This book may not be copied or reprinted for commercial gain or profit. The use of short quotations or occasional page copying for personal or group study is permitted and encouraged. Permission will be granted upon request. Scripture quotations are taken from the King James Version of the Holy Bible.

For Worldwide Distribution. Printed in the United States of America
Published by Jazzy Kitty Greetings Marketing & Publishing, LLC
Utilizing Microsoft Publishing and adobe software.

*Names have been changed in this book to protect their privacy and identities.

In Loving Memory Of

My Beautiful Grandmothers

Rev. Sarah H. Bryant

Mrs. Minnie L. Trammell

My Beautiful Godmother

Pastor Cynthia B. Duncan

My Dearest Friend

Christa Y. Harris

DEDICATIONS

To My Parents

Mr. Louis Trammell Sr. and Rev. Shirley Trammell

I am so thankful to God for He has chosen the two of you to be my parents before the foundation of the world. There were a lot of things that I didn't understand then, but troubles and trials have helped me to understand now. I love and honor you both very much.

To My Godparents

Apostle Bobby G. Duncan and the Late Pastor Cynthia A. Boyer- Duncan

You have been my foundation and you both have taught and instilled in me many things throughout my life. You were there when my birth was foretold and you knew the Destiny that God has for me. You saw how the enemy has tried to destroy my life and yet you still continued to love me through it all. I love you very much.

ACKNOWLEDGEMENTS

Anelda Ballard and Jazzy Kitty Publishing

I am so grateful for everything you have done and are continuing to do. You have been more than a friend, you are family.

September Summer

Words cannot express the gratitude that I have for you. Everything that you've done for me was done straight from your heart. Thank you for obeying God concerning me. You are truly a "God-send".

Apostle Patricia Smith

You have been and continue to be the "wind in my back". You have held my hand through the greatest of trials and tribulations. You have been more than a Spiritual Mother. I am eternally grateful to you.

Pastor Kim Davis

Thank you for your motherhood in my life. Thank you for pushing me beyond my limitations and making me to see that there is more for me. You gave me a chance when no one else thought I was qualified and you didn't give up on me.

ACKNOWLEDGEMENTS

Elders Rashan & Dean'a Robinson

I am thankful for the two of you more than you could know. The both of you have been there for me through some of my darkest hours. You have been there through prayer and you both have been a great encouragement. Thank you for being my "pillars". I love you both.

Caprice Love

You have seen me through all walks of my life and have continued to stand by me as a true friend. You loved me even when you didn't understand me. Thank you for the gift of true friendship. It is rare gem that I will continue to cherish. My love for you is great.

Alice Brazzle

You have been one of my biggest supporters from day one You encouraged me through every challenge and been brutally honest with me through everything. I am grateful to God for blessing me with a wonderful friend. I love you very much.

ACKNOWLEDGEMENTS

Peggy Vaughn-Bryant

I am so grateful to you for all of the love and support you have given me as my aunt. I am overwhelmed by everything you have done for me. It's my prayer that God richly blesses you in return. You have a heart of gold. I love you.

My Intermediate Family

You mean the world to me. I couldn't have asked for a better family. I am grateful for the bond that we share. Thank you all for supporting me and having my back. I love you.

My Extended Family

The Bryant Family, The Trammell Family, The Duncan Family and The Love-Maxwell Family; I wouldn't trade any of you for the world. You are all my true family and I love each and every one of you very much. If there is anyone that I may have overlooked, please charge it to my head and not my heart.

Last but not least, I want to thank God and my Lord and Savior Jesus Christ. For without Him I would not have a testimony.

Louis Trammell II

TABLE OF CONTENTS

INTRODUCTION i
CHAPTER 1 – CHILD OF DESTINY 01
   A New Sister 05
   Growing Pains 08
   A Baby Brother 13
CHAPTER 2 – TEENAGE TURBULENCE 16
   Kleptomaniac 18
   A Brush with Death 20
   My Other Family 23
   High School Drama 26
CHAPTER 3 – I'M COMING OUT 32
   Graduation 34
   He's Calling Me 36
   The Party Line 37
   13th Street 39
CHAPTER 4 – TEENAGER IN LOVE 43
   Star D'Amore 54
   The Break up 59
   Moving On 63
CHAPTER 5 – PARTY ANIMAL 68
   Return to 13th Street 69
   Me and My "Girls" 72
   A "Down Low" Affair 74
   Reconnecting with the Past 78
   To the Reader 80
ABOUT THE AUTHOR 82

FOREWORD

Pastor Kim A. Davis

Before I formed thee in the womb I knew [and] approved of you [as My chosen instrument], and before you were born I separated you; and set you apart, consecrating you; [and] I appointed you as a prophet to the nations. **Jeremiah 1:5 (Amp)**

The word **"destiny"** means *a predetermined course of events*. I believe the destiny of Louis Trammell was pre-determined before the foundation of the world and has already been set in motion.

His birth being prophesied beforehand and unexpected by his own mother; Louis was approved by God to be a chosen instrument to be used in this hour.

One of my favorite sayings is, "don't be moved by what you see, because what you see will mess you up". The early stages of Louis' life would mess up the mindset of the carnal eye. Truly it seemed to predict destruction. But the spiritual eye could see past the wrong turns and disasters of his life into a life that was destined for greatness.

I believe **"Destined To Do Damage"** is a life changing instrument predetermined by God to change the lives of what would otherwise be hopeless individuals.

How refreshing to see a young man who has chosen to use his life to help others rather than to mask it. I know you will be blessed by this awesome testimony.

INTRODUCTION

In the book of Joel, the Bible says that I will restore to you the years that the locust have eaten, the cankerworm, the caterpillar, and the palmerworm (Joel 2:25 KJV).

God has a way of restoring your life. Even when you feel like you have wasted your entire life. For years, I have always wondered what my life would have been like, had I not made the bad choices that I have made. Because of the call on my life, I should've been preaching the Gospel at the age of fifteen. But at the age of fifteen, I was a wild teenager doing everything that I was big and bad enough to do.

It's amazing how God doesn't change His mind concerning us. I had to find this out for myself. Several years ago, I was told through prophecy, that I would write a book about my life and that it will be a blessing to many. I never thought that I would write a book, especially one about my testimony. Whenever God reveals something to you that He wants to you to accomplish and it seems as though it is impossible, that's how you know it is God.

My story may be a little difficult for some to read about, be it must be told. Someone out there needs to read about it. God allowed me to go through the things that you will read about in this book so that He, and He alone will receive the glory. For years I have struggled with the "why me" syndrome. I blamed God for all of the things that He so graciously allowed me to go through and experience. God showed me that I had placed the blame on the wrong person and showed me my "real enemy".

The Bible says that we overcome by the blood of the lamb and by the words of our testimony (Rev. 12:11 KJV). A real testimony wields the power to break the powers of darkness off of another person's mind. Only God can deliver us out of the clutches of Satan and form us into vessels of honor. It is my prayer that my testimony blesses the lives of every reader for the glory of God.

CHAPTER 1

A Child of Destiny

"Before I formed thee in the belly I knew thee and before thou camest forth out of the womb I sanctified thee, and I ordained thee a Prophet unto the nations. Jeremiah 1:5 KJV

When I reflect back on my birth, it reminds me of how special to God I really must be. My mother and my Godfather have often told me about the prophecy which was spoken over my life before my mother even conceived me. That amazed me because it made me feel that I truly belonged to God, although most of my life, the devil has tried to make me feel the complete opposite.

I was told there was a Prophet from out town who was having a revival at the church which later became my home church. During the service, the Lord spoke through the Man of God and said there were two women who truly desired to have a baby, and there was one who didn't. By the time he said that, he was standing beside my mother's seat.

My mother told me during that moment she had said to herself, "I know he's not talking about me because I don't want any more children." At that time both of my sisters were in their pre-teens. The Prophet proceeded to call out the three women, one of them being my mother. My mother said that he looked at her and said, "I know you don't desire any more children, but the Lord has chosen you. You will birth a son and he will be a leader and a fighter for his people, and if you want to know who your son is, read the entire book of Joshua".

I can only imagine how my mother must've felt after that. She told me that she wasn't even pregnant when she received that word, but she wasn't surprised because of the way the spirit of the Lord flowed back in those days, with signs and wonders. There were a lot of family members and loved ones at the service who testified to the word that my mother received. She, my father and my two sisters had just moved into a nice home in the suburbs, and had settled down. My mother told me that there was an old saying "new house, new baby". How prophetic was that? The bible says in the book of Isaiah that God's word cannot return unto Him void, it must come to pass.

The following year I was born, Louis Junior to my parents. My sisters and I are thirteen years apart. It's a man's dream to have a son, and my father's dream came true. He was so proud when I was born, that he bought my mother a black mink coat and a diamond ring, and be bought cigars for all of his friends. Little did my father know that the devil had plans to destroy my life.

My parents were both hard workers who made good money, causing us to be a middle income class family, my father was a family man who always took care of us and did things with us as a family. My intermediate family was a "well to do" family. My sisters were called "the penthouse girls", due to the fact that my parents had money and my sisters had everything they wanted.

We were a happy family. Both of my parents had very well paid jobs and my sisters were the perfect 80's teen queens. They were involved in after school sports and many other activities. I was the pampered little brother that got just about everything I ever wanted. My sisters were my primary baby-sitters-which at times displeased them, especially my eldest sister. The girls were young and enjoying high school life in the mid eighties, they didn't want to be bothered with baby-sitting.

Nevertheless we were a close knit family. My father always had outings with us on the weekends. He loved the holidays and getting together with our relatives. My dad had a bar built in the basement of our home with a fresh supply of liquor. The basement of our home was his private den. He had it decked out with red carpet, fur rugs, a large pool table, a bar, an entertainment system and a dart board.

My father had a lot of parties in the basement which

consisted of both sides of my family and his friends. Since my mother was saved and heavily involved in my home church, she and her friends stayed upstairs and fellowshipped. I remember wanting to be where the "action" was, which was in the basement. I would sit in my room wearing my one piece pajamas with the foam footies plotting on ways to sneak past my mother to get downstairs.

I would sneak into the hallway and peak around the corner to see if my mother was around, and if her head was turned a certain way I would "zoom" downstairs. My aunts (my mother's sisters), taught me how to do particular dances. One of my aunts used to teach me how to do the "snake". This was a dance where you literally slithered around on the floor like a snake. I was the entertainment at these parties until my mother would drag me back upstairs.

I enjoyed my childhood growing up. Back then you didn't have the technology that we have available to us these days, so we rode our bikes, scooters and big wheels up and down the street. My neighborhood friends and I would ride our bikes and pretend every tree on our block represented one of our favorite fast food restaurants. We built clubhouses and lemonade stands. The ultimate electronic device to have back then was the original Nintendo system.

Me and my friends would get together and play Nintendo all day long, especially on Saturdays. We didn't have a care in the world. In my eyes, I had the "perfect" family and I was extremely happy, especially on the weekends when my father would take my mother and me out for the day. I always got to shop at my favorite toy store. My Dad took very good care of us and I loved him dearly.

My father was always the one taking hundreds and hundreds of pictures and spending time with us. People say that my mother spoiled me, but they're wrong, my father spoiled me terribly. He always held me and babied me, and he wouldn't let my mother reprimand me when I misbehaved. My father didn't know the damage he was doing to me by treating me like this. He made sure I had everything I wanted, which caused me to act out terribly when something didn't go my way.

A New Sister

As time progressed, my sisters graduated High School. My eldest sister went to the air force and the younger one went to College within the tri-state area. It was there that she met an intelligent, fun loving, born and bred Jamaican girl. She and my sister became very close friends and she told my sister all about her troubled past. My sister, (who is very compassionate), shared some things with my parents and they wanted to meet her. My mother and father loved the girl immediately and adopted her at the age of 20.

I was six years old at the time that I was introduced to my new sister. I loved her immediately and to this day I am grateful to God for bringing her into my life. My mother never treated her any different than she did my sisters. I was so excited to have a new member of the family even though she was the same age as my sisters. She was a major part of my life growing up and still to this day, she is my big sister. She is the "hilarious" one out of all of us and has kept us laughing for years. I couldn't imagine life without her. I was happy with my family life even though trouble within my family was brewing.

My mother did the best she could in raising me and bringing me up in the church. She and her eleven siblings were raised with a strong church background. Both of my mother's parents were Ministers of the Gospel. Mom had a rule in her household; you are to attend church without question until you turned eighteen. So, I was raised in a Pentecostal ministry, under the Leadership of my Godparents, where the spirit of the Lord moved mightily. My Godparents were both fervent preachers of the gospel and they lived by what they taught. I watched them cast out demons and prophesy and bring many people to Christ. This caused the foundation of the word of God to be planted in me at an early age.

The devil comes to try and steal the seed that has been planted in you by the Lord. Because he is a spirit, he has to use people to get to you. The call of God on my life is a militant one. The Lord called me to frontline ministry. This would require me to be a warrior in the spirit and when it comes to the devil, I am to take on the mentality of a serial killer. I know now that the enemy has plotted and planned as to how to destroy me. My family structure started to fall apart. My father loved me very much; but he and my mother were not getting along.

As a child I have witnessed the terrible arguments and fights they would have. This caused the spirit of fear to enter my life at a very young age. When my parents would fight, I would run and hide because fear would grip me strongly. I was very attached to my father. I remember that my father drove an orange Jeep Cherokee that you could hear a mile away, and I would wait by the window at night for my father to come home. My heart would leap when I heard that truck pulling into the driveway; but there were some nights when he didn't come home at all.

Let me pause here to remind you, this book is not a "tell all" book. The bible declares that we overcome by the blood of the lamb, and by the words of our testimony. I have made many mistakes in my life, but what the devil meant for bad, God has turned it around for my good. Some of the things that I share may be disturbing and shocking; but know that the hand of God was still over my life and He had a divine boundary around me. He allowed me to go through these experiences because He knew the people that He would use me to set free in His name. Let's get back to the story.

Growing Pains

As my parents marriage was falling apart rapidly, there were days when my father wouldn't come home. This caused a hole in my heart. By this time, my sisters were grown and out of the house. Many days it was just my mother and me. This was an open door for the enemy to plant an evil seed into my life. I thought that I was a normal boy until the kids in elementary school began to tell me differently.

I was told that I did things like a girl. We used to play a game in elementary school called "boys chase the girls", but something had to be wrong because I ended up running and screaming with the girls rather than chasing them. I was fascinated with dolls and girly things. Now the enemy found a way in, he had to hit me with full force. It was in the church where I was introduced to the spirit of Homosexuality. For the sake of privacy, I won't go into any detail, but I will say it felt so natural to me to be kissed and held by someone of the same sex. This all seemed so natural to me, and I remember the "butterflies" I would feel every time I was with the other person. Another bad seed was planted.

I began receiving this same kind of attention from other boys outside of the church; it felt normal to me to kiss a boy and put my arms around him the way a female would with a male. Back in the eighties we had a term for sex, we called it "bunning" or "humping". I wasn't even ten years old but I was "humping" with the boys in the basement of my home. This type of sex is what you would call "dry humping". I was a "bottom" before I knew what a "bottom" was. Whenever I was with a boy, I was treated like the "girl". The enemy's goal was to make me think I was a girl trapped in a boy's body.

Today, I thank God for His protection over my life. There was a boy who lived near me, and he was several years older than me. I would hang out with him at his house. There were times when I would be there with him when his family was not home, and it was during those times when he began to approach me sexually. He wanted to know what it would feel like to have sex with me. The first time he suggested it, I wasn't ready so we would just fondle and do other things. But one day in his uncle's den, he "wore me down", so to speak. We were there alone watching television and he approached me again. This time I gave in to him and it all felt so natural, but there was no penetration. I was eight years old at the time. Now the enemy had a foothold in my life.

My parents had no idea of the things I was doing and getting myself into. Things were so bad between them, that they didn't notice the perversion I was sucked into. To this day, I remember the very day my father walked out on my mother. I was sitting in the living room. My father came home and the next thing I knew, my parents were arguing. My father came out to where I was with my mother right on his heels. He kissed me on my forehead and told me he was leaving. I began to cry, and I begged him to stay, but he walked out anyway. After he left, I cried and cried. My whole world was crashing down around me. I was dealing with being teased at school every day, I suffered with asthma terribly, and my father just walked out on my mother, I was an emotional wreck.

Most people do not realize how real Satan is. Jesus told us in John 10:10 what the devil does. He comes to steal, kill and destroy. The fact that I was a little boy meant nothing to him. As far as he was concerned, he knew the damage I was destined to do to his kingdom; so he had to find a way to wipe me off the face of the earth. But, because God is who He is, the devil can only do to you what God allows him to do. The Lord, in His omniscience, knew that one day all of these experiences would create a powerful testimony. They would form into a bomb that God would throw at the enemy's camp to do DAMAGE!

I experienced traumas in my childhood that were designed to take me out of here. Experiencing homosexuality at such a young age, the constant teasing from my classmates, and my parent's divorce were devastating. However, the icing on the cake (so to speak) was when the love of my life, my grandmother went home to be with the Lord, after suffering with an illness. I was very close to my grandmother and had spent a lot of time with her prior to her illness. She affectionately called me her "Deacon". Like I said earlier, I was very close to my grandmother. She was my primary babysitter. At the time I was her youngest grandchild out of thirty (30) plus grandchildren. My grandmother would take me "uptown" everyday. "Uptown" consisted of shops and restaurants. "Uptown was right around the corner from my grandmother's house. We would go out for a walk everyday and I would come back with trinkets and gifts bought for me by my grandmother. She mostly purchased cross necklaces or chains for me from the religious book store that was around the corner. My grandmother knew my love for fried chicken and she would fry chicken for me sometimes in the morning, she and I called it "chicken right".

I remember how she would watch her favorite televangelists and when they would pray, she would have me join her by putting our hands on the television as in agreement with the prayer. My favorite thing to do at my grandmother's house was to feed the birds. My grandmother had a small slate out on the backyard just for feeding the birds. She was also a well known disciplinarian. She had a tree in her backyard, and if you got in trouble by her, she would have you go and get a "switch" (branch) off the tree and she would use it on you. I had many good memories of being at my grandmother's house and I loved her dearly. Knowing that I would grow up without her in my life was almost too much for me to bear. It would be years before the Lord actually healed me from the hurt of my grandmother's passing. The impact of these traumas caused me to follow a path of destruction.

A Baby Brother

After my father left and my parents were divorced, my mother became a single mother. My sisters were adults by this time and were starting families of their own, which left only my heartbroken mother and I. My father began to pay my mother Child Support and if I wanted to see him, I had to call him. Calling the Elks Home looking for my father became commonplace. I tried my best to maintain a close relationship with my father, until another reality slapped me in the face.

One particular day, my father picked me up because he had someone he wanted me to meet. He stopped at a particular house and had me follow him up the steps and into the house. I remember my father interacting with a baby. My father brought him to me and said, "This is your little brother". He was so adorable and innocent with the biggest "doe" eyes I had ever seen. He looked to be a year old because he was standing on his own, and I picked him up and held him. This made my father happy, and he felt that I was ready to meet his girlfriend.

I remember the day my father came to pick me up to spend the weekend with his family. I remember being very nervous because this was all new to me. When we got to my father's house, he opened the door and there was his girlfriend holding my brother on her lap, and sitting on the sofa. The meeting went well and she was always sweet to me. For the next several years, I would spend weekends with them. There were nights that I laid on the sofa bed wondering why this happened to me. Why was my father in the room with his girlfriend and new baby; and why was my mother out dating another man? The reality that my parents were never getting back together hit me like a ton of bricks.

The door was open for the enemy to whisper to me about my father having a "new family". I allowed rejection, bitterness and resentment into my heart at the age of eleven. I began to resent my father and his "new family". My anger separated me from my father and my brother; and I began to grow up with no father in my home. To prove the importance of having a father in the home, you should see the total difference between my brother and I, it would stagger you. He turned out extremely well. He is what you would call a "Jock". My father had him in sports since he was little. He is "all boy" with a good head on his shoulders. At the time of this writing, he will shortly be graduating high school.

Many, many times I have asked the Lord why I had to be the one without a father. For many years I wondered what my life would've been like if my father were totally in my life. It took me years to realize I was a little boy in a grown man's body seeking the attention of a man. I continued to grow up around a sea of women, which cause me to think like a girl, react like one and act like one. The hurt that I carried in my heart took me on a long roller coaster ride that led to many years of disappointment and hurt, on top of hurt and rejection. I hated my father for leaving me at such a young age. It hurt even more when he had another son that he did everything with. Even now, the two of them are very close and they spend a lot of time together.

For as long as I can remember, it has always been my heart's desire to have a father in my life. My search to fill that huge void has led to years of bad choices and a sinful lifestyle, but the Lord promises to restore the years that the cankerworm, palmerworm and locusts have eaten (Joel 2:25). Glory to God! Come on dear reader; let's continue on to the next chapter.

CHAPTER 2

Teenage Turbulence

Wherefore He is able also to save them to the uttermost that come unto God by Him, seeing He ever liveth to make intercession for them. Hebrews 7:25 KJV

As a teenager, I was complete mess. My manhood was completely gone, stolen by the devil. I never experienced what it was to think like a boy or behave like one. I was always feminine, and in my mind, I was female. Contrary to popular belief, homosexuality is a demonic spirit that is designed to destroy the God ordained family structure. This spirit is an abomination in the eyesight of God. This spirit found an opening in me when I was very little, and entered my body and grew up with me. That's why I never knew what it was to behave like a boy.

The spirit of effeminacy attached itself to the spirit of homosexuality. That means that the effeminate spirit became my very personality. All of this may sound far-fetched, but believe me demonic spirits are very real. Let me prove it to you in the scripture; *"For we wrestle not with flesh and blood, but against principalities, against powers, against the rulers of the darkness of this world, against spiritual wickedness in high places." Ephesians 6:12.*

We have all heard the phrase, "sticks and stones make break my bones but names will never hurt me", but that is a lie straight from the pit of hell. The bible says that the power of life and death is in the power of the tongue. I used to quote that "sticks and stones..." phrase when I was being teased. The words, "sissy", "cupcake", "little woman", "fruit" and "faggot" became word curses that were hurled at me for many years. Those words became seed that continued to grow and then reached full maturity. Most of the persecution came from males, which caused me to only be accepted by females. I have always been very comfortable around females; and I felt safe when I was with my "girls". They lashed back when boys would tease me in school, and wouldn't let anyone mess with me.

I was first introduced to masturbation in junior high school after lusting after my 7th grade shop teacher. Thoughts of pleasuring myself began to cloud my mind. I couldn't wait to get home to try out what I was seeing in my head. When I did that for the first time, I didn't know it would lead to years of perversion. I remember the first time I entered Intermediate High School, I got off the bus and went up the steps and through the lobby on my way to my 9th grade homeroom. As I walked through the hall, there was a boy I knew who was standing in the hallway with several other boys. He told them out loud to "watch out for "him", he's a faggot." That same boy also used to torment me all the time, prior to me entering Intermediate High School. I later found out that a group of kids used an Ouija board to find out if I was indeed gay.

Kleptomaniac

My school grades were so bad, that I ended up failing the ninth grade. However, though I failed the 9th grade, I was blessed to have 10th grade classes the following year. If I passed this time, I would go on to the 11th grade with my friends. During this time I took up the new "hobby" of stealing; and I was fifteen years old by this time. A group of us would leave school and catch the public bus to go to the mall and steal. This became a ritual. We got so good at stealing, that we would go to the mall with nothing but our lunch money and we would come back with bags of stuff. Because of my new hobby, I had all kinds of clothes, jewelry and other different things. This caused me to be popular with my peers. They were so amazed at how my friends and I could steal the way we did.

But soon it started to catch up with me. I was always in trouble at school, and was either suspended or on "I.S.S." (in school suspension). The Lord removed the grace off of my life and I found myself getting caught all the time. The next thing I knew, I found myself in a police station in a room handcuffed to a pole. The police were about to send me off to a youth detention center, but God in His mercy blocked it. That was the way He chose to deliver me from stealing. After that, if I even thought about stealing I would be afraid.

Reader, do you have a young loved one who is doing some of the things I was doing in school? Have you been praying and asking God for help? The best way to pray is to ask God to remove the grace off their life, but spare their life. I know that may sound a little harsh, but you have got to realize that the enemy is out to destroy your seed. God knows how to get their attention, trust me.

My teenage years were turbulent, many things happened to me. I had a sexual tryst with the only male friend I had at that time; and I remember when we were done, I felt so dirty, I hadn't been intimate with a boy since I was very little. The year was 1996 and I was 16 years old. I lusted after my friend for a long time; and I got to the point that I wanted him to know that I wanted to be with him. He too struggled with homosexuality, but he wasn't flamboyant like me. He secretly dealt with his struggle.

I made my feelings know to him by flirting with him. At first he would just push me away but finally he gave in. When it happened, there was no penetration. God truly protected me and wouldn't allow me to go as far sexually as I wanted to go. When it was over, my friend wanted me to stay and spend some time with him, but I had to get out of there. As I was leaving, he told me that he and an acquaintance of mine had been intimate. I was flabbergasted because the boy he was talking about was very manly and didn't appear to be gay.

On my way home I felt so dirty that I just cried and cried and begged God to forgive me. Back then I didn't know why I felt like that. Now I know the Lord was very disappointed with me and He allowed me to feel it. I ran to my cousin's house which was next door to me at the time, and I just cried and cried in her arms. It took a long time for me to face my friend again, and I just wanted to put what had happened between us behind me and move on.

A Brush with Death

I didn't know how much the devil really hated me until I got older, but at the age of 16, I had no clue. When I was little he tried to take me out with asthma. I had asthma really bad and I remember my mother taking me to the doctor's office over and over. I had to use an air machine to breathe. One night I had a severe asthma attack and I couldn't breathe. I had to blow air out of my mouth to breathe. On another night God supernaturally healed me at a service at my home church, Praise the name of the Lord.

While I was still 16 years old, the enemy tried again to wipe me out. This particular day I found myself in North Philadelphia, with two friends of mine. My friend Karla wanted to see her boyfriend who lived in the city. She knew that I loved to ride to the city, so she asked me to come with her. When she picked me up, she had another girl with her whom I knew from school. When we got to a particular area in the city, I didn't notice that it was a bad neighborhood. Up until that point, I had only been to the Center City section, where my sister lived.

Karla wanted to see her boyfriend for a little while, but I remembered we couldn't stay long because we had to pick up her mother from work. Karla's boyfriend had a gang of guys with him, and as we were leaving, I got into the backseat of the car. One of the guys took the other girl down the street to talk to her. Little did I know that this was a set up to keep her away from me so the other guys could attack me. I remember fear gripped me hard as I sensed something was wrong.

All of sudden, one of the guys came to the backseat,

punched me in my face, and snatched off the gold herring bone chain my father bought me for Christmas. Then more of them came in the car to attack me. One of them asked me what my shoe size was; I knew he was going to ask me to take off my white patent leather sneakers, so I had to think very fast. I lied and told him they were a size 9, and he immediately punched me in my face.

I began to scream for help, and suddenly Karla opened the other side of the back door closet to the side I was on. She grabbed my legs because the guys were trying to pull me out of the car. They finally gave up with the struggle and tried to beat me up as much as they could in the car. By this time, the other girl that had come with us was running up the street to the car. One of the men pulled a gun out. I shudder to think what could've happened if they had gotten me out of the car. Karla and the other girl got in the car, and Karla got us out of there as fast as she could.

I praise God for covering me and protecting me. My life could've ended at the age of 16 years old, but like the songwriter says, "God blocked it". It's very hard reliving the testimony as I write this. Hell could've been my home if that man would've shot me. I am so thankful for God's mercy and His grace. He is so awesome.

Karla and the other girl kept apologizing to me. Karla had no idea that they were plotting to attack me; but she said the thing that triggered it was fact that I had on jewelry and nice clothes. They would've killed me for that. When we got back to Coatesville to pick up Karla's mother, Karla told me to hide my face from her mother because she didn't want her mother to know what took place and where we were hanging out. My face was swollen, with a broken nose and a black eye.

When I got home, I told my mother I was mugged; and she came busting out of her bedroom and into my room where I was. She cried as she cupped my face in her hands, and kept asking me what happened. I was angry with my mother during that time because she was in a relationship with a man that I hated at the time. I was a confused and messed up boy, but the Lord still had to keep His word concerning my life. He still loved me regardless of everything I was getting myself into. I truly know that when God speaks a word concerning your life, the devil CANNOT touch you until that word has come to pass.

My Other Family

I was so shook up from the attack, that I feared the city itself. Afterwards, even when my family would go to visit my sister in Center City, I was terrified. It would take several years before God rid me of that fear. I remember the Sunday after the attack; I still had to go to church with a black eye and everything. I remember going into my Godfather's office after church. He took one look at me and asked me what happened. The rest of the family came in to see me and also wanted to know what happened. They were truly concerned for my life. My Godparents knew what the enemy was trying to do, but they wanted me to know if for myself. My Godsister said that I was blessed growing up because I had two families.

Apart from my natural immediate family, I had my Pastor's family. My Pastor was my Godfather, and was the only consistent male figure that I had growing up. He spent as much time as he could with me, although he was a very busy man. He referred to me as the son he never had, and I was always with the "First Family". I went on trips and hung out with his daughters (my Godsisters) often. Every Sunday I went out to eat with my Godparents.

I remember how my Godfather would walk my Godmother to the car, open her door and make sure she was in before he would shut the door. My Godmother would immediately put her seatbelt on. And my Godfather would get in the car and start to drive. Then the inevitable would happen, he would say, "Pea (my nickname), tell me what I preached about today"? I would sink in my seat because in those days, I was a silly teenager in church. It was hard to pay attention to the word because the teenagers would have a ball writing notes, sneaking out of church to go to the store, and playing "hooky". My Godmother would always come to my rescue by finishing my sentences for me.

I loved them so much, and now that I'm a grown man, I see that God kept me close to such awesome Pastors for a reason. My Godfather was a "jokester", but this was a side of him that you rarely saw in public. I can never forget how my Godmother would pull me to the side and say "don't forget to ask Pastor how much you're worth". (How much your meal is going to be). We would start to order and I would say, "Dad, how much and I worth?", and he would say "a glass of water". Yes, truly I was blessed to have them in my life.

Because my father wasn't around, I tried to put my Pastor in my father's place. This became detrimental to me because he couldn't possibly spend the time with me that I wanted. There were times I felt as if he was rejecting me, just like I felt my father did. This caused me to "act out" even more. Yet and still, throughout my life, this family has always received me, no matter how the enemy as tried to separate me from them. That's real love.

High School Drama

By the time I entered Senior High School, everybody knew I was gay, and I didn't go through a lot of teasing anymore. By this time I was respected for being so "openly gay". Back at my church home, I was the youth ministry's first president. This ministry was headed by my Godmother, who was very passionate about the youth and their salvation. She had a staff that consisted of her three daughters and a few other adults in the ministry. We had meetings and went on trips, but the "highlight" of every month was our Friday night shut-ins. We would spend the night as the church, and fellowship. We had food, fun and fellowship, but the main purpose was for us to draw closer to God and to know Him.

During a particular shut-in, we were sitting in a circle having a serious discussion, before we went into prayer. Then, as different ones found a space in the room to go and talk to God privately, I remained next to my Godmother. I remember laying my head on her leg, and then she came out and confronted me about living a homosexual lifestyle. She did this in love, and made sure that no one but she and I could hear. I was shocked because I had never talked to her about this before. She had tears in her eyes when she confronted me about it. She was concerned for my life, but she knew that God had the last say.

My Godmother would not let my outward appearance and actions deter her from what God said concerning my life.

Prior to my Godmother confronting me, I was angry with my Godfather (Pastor), because I was feeling neglected by him. I wanted to hurt him like I felt he had hurt me. After service one Sunday, I strutted up to him as he was about to enter into his office and I said to him "Dad, I'm a homosexual...a Big one" and I strutted back down the hall. As I walked away, I felt pleased with myself, not knowing that the enemy was using me to destroy my connection to the Pastor.

Back in school, I was wild, and much bolder than I had ever been. The friends that I was with were the ones I grew up with since elementary and junior high school, and they were all girls. My grades were so bad that I was placed in the "L.D." (Learning Disabled) classes. Even with being in the "L.D." classes, my grades didn't improve that much. I will never forget when my Guidance Counselor came to a particular class I was in and began to announce our GPA's (Grade Point Average). When she got to my name, she didn't announce it but whispered "1.2" in my ear. I cannot forget how my heart dropped when she told me that. I began to believe that I was stupid. I didn't know how to study and would become so frustrated with school work, that I began focusing on partying with my peers, and chasing after a certain boy.

I began to grow strong feelings for a particular boy that I knew from school. This all started at a New Year's Eve Party, when I noticed that he "responded" to me differently than the other boys did. The night I saw him at the party we spoke to each other and he put his hand on my lower back. I immediately began to feel those "butterflies". It was as if something sparked in me. After that party, I began to plot on how to "get" this boy to like me the way I liked him. I didn't know then that the choices that I would make to pursue this guy would result in major damage to my character and reputation.

You may ask, "What would cause you to chase after a boy in school like this? Why?" He gave me the attention that I craved from a male. Whether he knew it or not, he filled the "void" in my life that craved male attention. I thought of ways that I could attract him to me. I began to change the way I dressed. I went from jeans and sneakers to dressier clothing. I started to have my eyebrows arched and my hair colored. In my mind, as far as I was concerned, I was a girl. So what do "girls" do when they really like a boy? They tell their friends.

My opportunity to tell the girls came when I hosted a birthday party for one of them at my house. It was just our "clique" and I decided to officially tell them that I was indeed gay and that I had strong feelings for this particular guy. This was a bad move on my part because in reality, I was a boy telling seven girls that I was in "love" with another boy. That made for good gossip. Out of those seven, two were my closest friends. Those two were the ones I grew up with from elementary school. I remember when I told them that I was gay; the eyes of both of them teared up; and they said they were proud of me that I "came out"

However, this is when I began to experience betrayal. When I told the girls, they promised that it wouldn't leave that room. But in every group, there is a "motor mouth". After I told my true confession, I continued to pursue the boy that I was infatuated with. I would ride my friend's school bus home and go to her house every day. Then later we would venture into town where the guy lived, so that I could see him. One particular day my friend and I were walking in town and he rode pass us in his car. When he saw us, he beeped the horn; and my friend waved but I didn't. I used that opportunity to "test" him to see if he would respond to me the way that I wanted him to.

As he and his friend drove around the corner, my friend and I went into the corner store. My heart leapt when he walked into the store. He asked me what was up and why I didn't wave to him when he rode by. My plan had worked. He said that we should all get together and go out some time and then he left. I couldn't believe that he parked his car with his friend sitting in there to come and speak to me. These things didn't happen to someone like me. I just knew that he liked me, and with my friend being there to witness this, she also was convinced that he liked me. I was so excited that I told my other "girlfriends".

All of a sudden, classmates would walk up to me in school and ask me if I liked this guy; and say they heard that he and I were going out to eat and different other things. I was horrified and hurt that one of my friends began talking. The gossip spread like a "wildfire", and not just in the school, but also around the city. This caused the boy to back away from me, which resulted in heartbreak for me. He never came off as though he was "gay" but the attention he gave me caused me to wonder. In my mind, he was my boyfriend, and I couldn't stop thinking about him. By now people were coming up to him asking him questions.

Some of the guys that I was "cool" with stopped speaking to me, and began shunning me. I couldn't believe how the gossip had spread. At that time, the guy was popular and an excellent basketball player, with a basketball scholarship waiting on him. After the gossip, when he did see me, he was very cordial to me, but there was a major difference from how we previously would interact. I was grateful that he was still kind enough to speak to me, but sad that I no longer would receive the attention that I needed from him. This added to the wound of rejection in my life; which caused me to act out even the more.

CHAPTER 3

I'm Coming Out!

Thou shalt not lie with mankind as with womankind: it is an abomination. Leviticus 111-22 KJV

Graduation was fast approaching which meant that our Senior Prom was right around the corner. In our town, the Prom is a major event. Many people come to see you get out of the car, and walk around taking pictures before you walk into the school. I loved to design and my friends knew it. One of my friends had me to design her gown, which turned out very nice.

Because my personality was very flamboyant, it meant that my outfit, as well as that of my date's, had to be flamboyant. I took my cousin and a friend of mine to the Prom. I designed very revealing outfits for each of us that were made out of gold crochet yarn. The girls wore two differently designed gold crochet dresses with a white leather bra and shorts underneath. One wore a blonde hairstyle and the other, a black one. I wore a white satin jacket and pants, with a gold crochet tank top underneath. The jacket had the gold crochet on the collar, belt and cuffs.

My pants were "out" (open) on both sides with gold lace on

them. The girls wore white feather flocks to "cover up" the revealing dresses. I had my hair dyed golden blonde. My father helped my mother and my aunt to pay for my outfit (which was very expensive).

However, he refused to come and see me after he heard of me dying my hair blonde, and wearing this flamboyant outfit. My father heard about the rumors of the lifestyle I was living, and he refused to come see me off to the Prom.

I remember when the girls came to pick me up in a white Lexus. I got in the car and began to sip on the liquor that we had. I began to drink because I was nervous. I knew that the area would be packed outside of the school, with people. When we finally pulled up in front of the school, the girls got out of the car first. I took a deep breath and got out of the car. As soon as I got out, the crowd went wild as I "sashayed" around while people took pictures of the girls and me. One look at my outfit, my hair and the way I acted, you immediately knew that I was a homosexual. After my Prom, I became a local "celebrity", and kids and young people would run up to me screaming, "You're the boy from the Prom". Plus, the dresses I designed became "trendsetters" in future Proms in our area, and many girls dressed in more revealing dresses. To this day, people are still talking about my Prom.

Graduation

After my triumph at the Prom, it was time to prepare for my graduation. I found out that I was "allowed" to graduate with my class. In normal cases if you had a 1.2 grade point average, that's immediate failure. Nevertheless I was extremely excited about my graduation. It meant that I didn't have to go back to school anymore. But I had no plans after High School. I had no college or trade school to attend, or good paying job to go to. I hadn't planned for my future because partying with my "girls", chasing after boys, and looking cute were my main priorities.

My friends had colleges, trade schools and jobs to attend, but I didn't. I was a wounded and rebellious teenager with a bad attitude. The devil was having a field day with my life and I seemed to be going downhill. On the day of my graduation, I had a bad argument with my mother; resulting in my father calling me and threatening to "kill" me if I ever disrespected my mother again. He had hurt me once again. I had never heard my father talk to me like that before. However, what he said on the phone to me didn't compare to the damage he did to me later in the day.

My mother and I made up from our argument as we prepared for the ceremony. Days prior to this, the students received a form asking us how we wanted our names to be announced at the ceremony. Now anyone that really knows me knows that I dislike my middle name, but I knew my father would come to my graduation and I want him to be proud of me. So I requested that my entire name be announced.

When the time came for me to receive my diploma, I was so happy. I knew my family was out in the crowd cheering me on.

However the ceremony was over and I found out my father hadn't attended my graduation, I was crushed. Even more so, when I found out he took his girlfriend and their son to Disneyland the very day of my graduation, I was devastated. On the table at home were three cards for me from my father. Each had a one hundred dollar bill inside of it. That money could not replace the hurt and rejection I felt from his absence. This gave the enemy room to whisper hatred in my ear towards my father.

By this time, I hated him for skipping my graduation to take his son to Disneyland. My father was at both of my sister's graduation ceremonies, taking pictures of them. He will most definitely be there for my brother's graduation but he did not attend mine. It took years before I was able to forgive him. For the summer of 1998, I smoked marijuana and cigarettes, and I drank beer and liquor like a fish until the entire three hundred dollars was spent.

He's Calling Me

In the fall of 1998, I began to feel the Lord tugging at my heart. I knew that it was time to come back to Him. By this time, I was 18 years old. After returning back to the Lord, I threw away all of my "worldly music". Let me pause here to say that God deals with His children differently in His relationship with each one, and the way He chooses to deliver us. Certain music connected to my past made me think of things that were not of God. If I continued to listen to those music tapes, I would've eventually found myself back out in the world

It takes sacrifice to draw closer to God. It calls for you to get rid of things that might mean the world to you. To receive deliverance, sometimes you have to take drastic measures. I found myself in that church building every time the door opened, but I still struggled with perversion. It didn't matter how many times I was prophesied to, or how many times I was called up to the front to get prayed for. My Pastor (Godfather) would call me up to the front, and the intercessors and ministers would crowd around me and Pastor would scream in my ear, "come out Satan, loose your hold", "COME OUT!" Quite a few preachers had tried to do this same thing to no avail.

The amazing thing to me was the fact that the call of God on my life was very visible to the spiritual eye; but the same time;

I was outwardly struggling to find my identity and to become free from a life of perversion. I still continued to draw close to God the best way I knew how. I will never forget the day I received the Holy Spirit. It was shortly after I gave my life back to the Lord. It was Friday night prayer service at my home church. One of the intercessors told me that the Holy Spirit was hovering over me, but that He wanted to live inside of me. I could feel this tingling feeling all over me.

When I went home, I remember being nervous because I had never experienced anything like that before. I sat in the basement and I invited the Holy Spirit into my life that night. All of sudden, I began to quicken (see Romans 8:11), and I heard this language in my ear. I didn't want my mother to hear me so I began to whisper what I heard. It was an awesome experience and I knew that I was well on my way to a closer relationship with the Lord. When the enemy sees that you are drawing closer to God, it is his job to cut you off and separate you from God. And how does he do that? He uses people. In my case, he used an acquaintance of mine who was outwardly gay, to draw me back out into the "world"

The Party Line

This acquaintance quickly became a new friend. And before

I knew it, I found myself back out in the "world". I never had a gay male friend before, and we had the time of our lives together. We were like "girlfriends". We went shopping and out to eat, just like normal girlfriends did. One day he introduced me to the "party line". This was a number you would call to meet other gay men, to connect with them and possibly date them. I became so hooked on this that I purchased my own phone line in the house. I couldn't wait to get home from work to call the party line and meet other men.

To me, it was exhilarating to be able to freely talk to a man who was interested in getting to know me. I'd meet quite a few men outside of the party line; but I now had boys to talk to and flirt with. I remember that I would have to find a private place to talk on the phone. The party line was what the enemy used to draw me further away from the Lord. The bible says in the book of James, Chapter 1 verse fourteen and fifteen (James 1:14-15), *"But every man is tempted, when he is drawn away of his own lust, and enticed. Then when lust hath conceived, it bringeth forth sin. And sin when it is finished, bringeth forth death."* I was drawn away from the Lord because of the desires that *were* still in my heart. Soon, the party line was not enough for me anymore; I was now ready to take this to another level. My new "friend" and I began to venture down to the city to meet the men.

13th Street

Thirteenth Street was an area in Philadelphia where many homosexuals, lesbians, drag queens and transsexuals would congregate. You either came alone to get a "date", or you come with your friends to hang out. Clubs were on every corner, but it was really "live" when all of the clubs closed for the evening. I was 18 years old when I was first introduced to this area, which I had heard about, and I was anxious to get down there to see what it was like.

I first went there with an older gay man whom I knew by acquaintance. This particular man was a "hermit". He didn't hang out in the public and I found that out the hard way. When we got there, I was excited to see all of the people hanging out and I was anxious to get out and walk around. But, the man I was with kept driving around the block, over and over again until he caught the eyes of a man who was much younger. He told me to get in the back, so this "mystery man" could sit in the front.

What my acquaintance was doing is what you would call "cruising". Cruising is defined as "checking out somebody". Once you get that's person's attention, you give that person a look which "invites" them to come over to you and "hook up". My acquaintance began to drive seeking a secluded *area* in the city. Once he found a spot that seemed to be private, he told me to get out of the car for a few minutes, and stand away from the car. I had no idea what was going on until it finally hit me that my acquaintance was being "serviced" by this man. I was horrified! After a few minutes, the man got out of the car and left. When I got in the car, I was disgusted and disappointed as my acquaintance proceeded to drive me back home, (which was about an hour away from the city). I never contacted him again.

The next time around, I was accompanied by my new "friend", "Kyle", who was young and ready to meet guys and have fun. We became regulars to 13th Street, where we were meeting new people and making friends. The main club on 13th Street had a "youth night" every Wednesday, and you had to be 18 or older to get in. I was in that gay club every Wednesday night with my friend Kyle. But the "action" didn't happen until the club let out. The streets would be packed with men and a few women.

The alley between 13th Street and Locust Street held a lesbian club and an Adult bookstore right around the corner; and there was another gay bar right beside the Lesbian club. That particular bar was very strict about I.D., and it would be a little over a year before I could enter that particular bar. 13th Street was the place to be. One particular night, Kyle picked me up at my house and I noticed that he was with someone. His name was Dion. Dion and I became fast friends, and the three of us became the best of friends. We did everything together. When we came down to 13th Street, we had the times of our lives.

I remember how on 13th Street, late at night, the "down low brothers" would drive around the block looking for some "action". We would be standing on the corner looking our best and a guy would drive by. If he liked what he saw, he would continue to drive around the block until he caught your eye. Once the two of you made eye contact, he would pull in a private area to talk to you. This has happened to me many times. It became normal to walk down 13th Street with my friend, and have guys grab me to try to talk to me. I can still hear the men saying, "Yo, baby let me talk to you for a minute", and some men were very persistent.

I loved all the attention that I received. It made me feel attractive (I had always thought I was ugly), and it made me feel wanted. Now that I look back, it's amazing how the grace of God has kept me when I was in the city late at night gallivanting and looking for a man to want me. God is so awesome. His love and grace still covered me while I was living a lifestyle that was an abomination right before His eyesight. Though I was living the homosexual lifestyle at such a young age, there was still a divine boundary around me and there were some things that God in His mercy would not allow me to do.

CHAPTER 4

A Teenager in Love

And likewise also the men, leaving the natural use of the women, burned in their lust one toward another; men with men working that which is unseemly, and receiving in themselves that recompense of their error which was meet. Romans 1:27 KJV

I was 19 years old when I became a regular on 13th Street. My friends and I drove down just about every night. Dion and Kyle were both seniors in High School, and I was a graduate. It was perfect for me because at that time I was collecting unemployment and had no real responsibilities. I remember Dion and I would go shopping at the mall to find something to wear just to parade around 13th Street.

I was having so much fun with my friends and my new hangout spot, that thoughts of the Church were far behind me; but I could never stop thinking about God. One night we were on our way to 13th Street, and Dion's tire went flat as soon as we got there. He pulled into one of the alleys and went looking for help. Dion came back with a man who looked to be no older than 40 years old. He was very nice to us and he put on the spare tire for us; as he was replacing the tire he wanted to know how much we would pay him for his services. We didn't have much money on us at the time so he said that he wanted ME for payment instead.

I remember the fear that gripped me when he said that. He was dead serious. As he was fixing the tire, he would keep referring to how he and I were going to "get it on" after he was done. To look at this man, you would have never known he was a homosexual. That's just how "manly" he was, and he was tall and well built. I began praying (in my head), asking the Lord to protect me from this man and to make a way for us to get out of this situation without either one of us getting hurt. When he finished replacing the tire, he "suddenly" had a change of heart, and asked Dion for just a ride instead.

We were all very relieved because if we had to, we would have fought him if he had become violent. The Lord answered my silent prayer in His mercy. It's amazing how He cared for me and protected me during those times. Even during those times when I was "out there", I spent time at home and frequently attended church. I received a prophecy that the eyes of the Lord were watching me and following me everywhere I went. I never forgot that prophecy. Through that prophecy, God in essence, was telling me that He still loved me and He was protecting me.

Dion was from a church background like me. He told me

one night that while he was in a church service in our hometown, there was a Preacher from out of town ministering. The minister called out my mother and told her that God said not to worry about your son, and that he (I) was covered under the blood of Jesus. I can only imagine how worried my mother must've been for me during that time.

I was in Philly late at night, and didn't come home until the wee hours of the morning sometimes. It's awesome how one word from the Lord can cause you to have peace about severe situations. I knew my mother and other loved ones were praying for me. They knew that the enemy was out to kill me and get rid of me before God could deliver me and raise me up, but the prayers of the righteous have availed much!

At that time in my life it was refreshing for me to actually have friends that I could relate to. Up until that time it's been all girls. My new best friends and I could freely tell each other about who we liked and what we would do to get his attention. We shopped together and hung out just like good "girlfriends" would do. We would go to the Mall just to buy outfits to hang out on 13th Street. We were there almost every night. For years up until this particular time; I have watched how guys would hit on my girlfriends and how my girlfriends would act in response to them, now I began experiencing how it felt to be "hit on".

The feeling was exhilarating to me. There were times when we would be walking around 13th Street and men would try to talk to me and get my attention. Dion and Kyle always handled attention like champions. I remember one particular night we were hanging out as we were walking a car pulled up in front of us and this guy asked Kyle if he could talk to him and Kyle jumped in front seat and they drove off.

Dion and I could not believe how fearless Kyle could be at times. But knowing him as we did, we knew he would catch up with us. Dion and I continued on walking and having conversation as we turned the corner, there were guys hanging out on the stoop. As we passed by not paying them any mind, one guy cut right into a conversation that I was having with Dion. He actually answered the question that I had asked Dion which caused us to stop and see the person that flirtatiously interrupted us.

His name was "Dante". I knew that Dante was interested in Dion so I backed up so that they could talk which caused me to have light conversation with Dante's friends. Dante said that we should hang out at a different location. Dion and I got in his car and we followed Dante and his friends. Dion loved to blast music in his car, especially when he played his favorite song, so he put on his song and began to drive faster. Like a champ,

Dion knew how to flirt and drive at the same time, which is what he and Dante were doing as we were heading to our location. Dion and Dante began racing each other and clowning around. We had a "ball" hanging out with Dante and his friends. We ended up in the location of an "underground" gay club that most "thug" types hung out in.

Because Dion and I were underage, we didn't even try to go in. The gay bars/club scene was very strict on identification and being of age. So we hung out with Dante outside of the area for awhile. Before he went in the club to join his friends he got Dante's phone number and we left to meet Kyle back on 13th Street. We finally met back up with Kyle and we got to meet his new friend. Little did we know that this "friendship" between Kyle and his new friend would evolve into a very intense love relationship. I was the one who was still single. My friends used to tell me that I was a "tease". I would flirt with men and keep on moving. I had not yet experienced a real relationship with another man but that all changed sooner than I thought.

I encountered three relationships out of my experiences on 13th Street. The three men that I dated were "straight appearing" men. In each relationship, I was the "female role" or "bottom". The first young man I dated name was Marlon. He was 24 years old and I was 19 years old at the time. I would see Marlon around when I began frequenting 13th Street. Kyle told me that Marlon had been watching me for quite some time. Marlon began inquiring about me to Kyle and I had no idea until Kyle told me. Marlon was your typical "thug" in his appearance. He wore the bandanas, the t-shirts and baggy jeans, the timberlands and the "doo-rags". You would have never known that Marlon was gay. I remember the night that Marlon got the "courage" to approach me. On this night, Kyle and I were hanging out. I was in the pizza shop while Kyle was outside on the strip hanging out.

When I walked outside of the shop Kyle motioned for me to come over to where he was. He was talking to some guys in a vehicle. As I crossed the street I realized that Marlon was in the vehicle with his friend. Marlon asked me for my telephone number and flooded me with compliments. He made it known to me that he was interested in getting to know me more. He said he would call me and flashed a mega watt smile. As I walked away I was ecstatic, but I wouldn't let him see it. We began seeing each other and things were okay until I noticed that something was "off".

I couldn't put my finger on it at the time but I knew something wasn't right. On my way to the mall with Dion and

Kyle on one particular afternoon, I decided to ask Marlon what was going on. I reached from the back seat and grabbed Dion's phone and called Marlon. Like I mentioned earlier I was the "female role" in the relationship; and I played that role to the max. I began complaining to him about him not spending enough time with me and other things. He said that nothing had changed. I immediately believed him and felt relieved as he assured we were fine. Little did I know the "surprise" I would receive later on that evening. Marlon said he would meet me on 13th Street later that night and he gave me a particular time. My friends and I got there a little early and we were hanging out and talking to some of our Philly friends. I began wondering if Marlon would really show up, but he finally did and he strolled around the corner with an acquaintance of mine. I wondered what Marlon was doing with him because I had never seen those two together before. Marlon seemed a little distant and I was trying to figure out why. I got my answer when I was chatting with my acquaintance.

I asked him how did he know Marlon and he said that he and Marlon were together and have been for years. I couldn't believe Marlon "played" me like he did. I walked away from my acquaintance with Kyle and another friend of mine on my heels. My friends confronted my acquaintance and he said he had no idea about my relationship with Marlon. I was ready to go home because I didn't want to face Marlon. My friends told me that when they confronted him, he downplayed our relationship status to "just friends". I found out what it meant to be "played".

After sulking for several days, Dion and Kyle brought me back to my senses. They told me it was time for me to move on. I agreed and began hanging out again in Philly. I would not see Marlon for quite some time. Back then, I believed that in order to move on from a man was to date another. I began seeing another Man but it wasn't serious. I kept my guard up with him due to my past experience with Marlon.

I already knew what this particular guy was about. He was very tall and extremely built and he was manly and had a laid back type of personality. He and his friend spotted Kyle and I while we were out on the strip one night. He and his friend walked over to us and began talking to us. He made it known that it was me that he was interested in.

My interest in this man didn't last very long, in fact it ended on the day that I met the next man I became involved with, "Rick". By the time Rick came into my life, Dion, Kyle and I were pretty popular around 13th Street. People knew who we were and we made many connections. The night I met Rick, me and my friends were hanging out. Prior to this time I had not seen or heard from my "friend" that I was seeing in awhile and it didn't really bother me that much.

There were some acquaintances that we were hanging out with who were friends with Rick. Through them I heard little about Rick. I was interested in getting to know him, but I didn't chase after him. When I finally saw Rick, I was even the more interested, but I played the coy role. He played into it, and it was very obvious to everyone around us that we were very attracted to each other.

I was set on making Rick mine. As the evening progressed, and we all were having a good time, my "friend" (the guy I was seeing), pops up out of nowhere (so to speak). I was a little annoyed that he picked this particular time to show up. He began laying "claim" on me by putting his arms around me and trying to kiss me. I knew he was a little "tipsy". I kept pushing him away but he wouldn't give up that easy.

It was as if he knew that Rick was interested in me and he wasn't having it. I could tell by the look on Rick's face that he was confused about what was going on. I knew I had to make a decision and a quick one at that. I told my "friend" that "whatever" we had was over. I didn't want to be with someone whom I barely saw.

I explained to Rick the situation and he understood. He still wanted to get to know me. I was elated as we exchanged numbers. Rick had a "pager" (before mobile phones ruled the world, pagers were very popular). Around this time, mobile phones just starting becoming popular and pagers were becoming extinct. Rick gave me his pager number and his home number. Rick treated me differently from the other guys. He was playful, attentive and passionate. Whenever I called his pager he would immediately respond, even if he was at work. I loved that about him.

One night I remember Dion taking me to see Rick at his job. We were becoming a couple and it was happening very fast. I couldn't wait to get to Philly just to see him and spend time with him. I was falling in love head first with Rick. During this time, my Godfather had a preaching engagement in Atlanta Georgia for the weekend and I had planned to join him, just to spend some time with him because I hadn't done so in awhile. This was prior to Rick and I becoming a couple. I tried to back out but my Godfather made me come with him. There were a couple of men from the church who were joining us as well. I was livid with my Godfather. I just wanted to stay and be with Rick.

During my flight to Atlanta, all I thought about was Rick

and my friends and wondering what they were doing. I would call Rick from the hotel a couple of times during that weekend. I missed him terribly and I couldn't wait to get back home to see him and my friends. During this trip to Atlanta, I was elated to see my favorite uncle (on my father's side) and my aunt. They had moved to Atlanta years before. My aunt (who is a Woman of God), began to prophesy to me and told me that there was some things that I was involved in and people that I needed to stay clear from. She said that she would name them to me. I told her I already knew.

I was a "mess" and it was very clear that I was a homosexual. I even wore blue colored contacts during this visit to Atlanta. The devil had my mind and I knew he did. I understood what my aunt said to me prophetically, but it wasn't time for me to come out of what I was caught up in as of yet. Sometimes you or the person that you've been praying for has to go through the things that they are in because God is building up a testimony for you or your loved ones.

For God to get the glory, there must be a story. Don't give up praying and believing for yours or your loved one's deliverance. The process can take a very long time as it has in my case. But know that God is the deliverer and in His timing He will bring you out as long as you remain faithful to Him.

Now back to the story. I wasn't ready to let go of my lifestyle. To me, the "fun" was just beginning. I had a "man" and a life to get back to and I was elated about the fact that I was leaving the next day to go home. I actually ended up enjoying my time in Atlanta with my Godfather and some of the people that were with us.

When our plane began to land in Philadelphia, I was so excited I could've jumped up and down inside of the airplane. I was so happy to see Rick and my friends, you would've thought I'd been gone for months. My relationship with Rick was going well at that time and I couldn't have been happier, but that would soon change.

Star D'Amore

Rick was the leader of a "House". These were actually different cliques that each had a "Leader" and a "1st Lady". This was a major thing in the homosexual community. In a "House" you had to be able to "vogue" and you had to be very good at it. You also had to be a good dancer and you absolutely had to have style. Once a year there would be an annual "Ball", where the different cliques or "Houses" would compete. They would be judged on how well they could vogue, style and dance. In these "Houses", the Leader and the 1st Lady had to be the absolute best in each category.

In this case, Rick was definitely qualified to be the Leader. Rick's clique was up and coming, and the newest "House" to the community. This is around the time I met him. Rick named the "House' D'Amore (which was his mother's maiden name). Rick and I become an exclusive couple quickly. Up until this time, I was the single one in my circle of friends (Dion and Kyle were both in serious relationships).

Because Rick was the Leader of the "House of D'Amore", I was in a relationship with him, which made me the "1st Lady". In a "House", that was the most glamorous position to hold. After I was explained to about the position and what it entailed, I knew I didn't have what it took to carry the position. I didn't think I would be able to be what Rick and the "D'Amore" crew expected me to be, but Rick had plans to change all of that.

Dion happened to be dating Rick's best friend Aaron. Aaron lived right around the corner from Rick in North Philadelphia. Aaron's house became the hangout spot for the "D'Amore" crew. It was there that we practiced "walking the runway" and how to vogue and do other routines. Aaron's mother and siblings became like family to the "D'Amore" crew. She never judged us and she let us stay in her home as long as we wanted. The D'Amore "House" had quite a few members and we began to connect like a family.

Out of all of us (male and female) that were a part of D'Amore, Aaron's mother really took to Dion and Me. I believe it was because Dion was in a relationship with her son (Aaron) and me with Rick, (whom she treated like a son). My relationship with Rick was well known around 13th Street. When people saw me, they knew whom I belonged to and vice versa. Once Rick and I became an exclusive couple, he became set on changing my image. One particular late night, Rick rode back to my hometown with Dion and I. There were times when Rick would ride back home with us and stay at Dion's house. Rick drove Dion's car while Dion slept in the back seat.

Rick pulled up in front of my house and said to me very seriously that now that I was a 1st Lady of a "House", I needed to get rid of my mustache. This shocked me because I never really paid attention to my mustache. I had never shaved it off and I was nervous about what I would look like without it. I knew that in several hours, he would be back to pick me up to take me back to Philly with him so I didn't have much time to think about this. By the time Rick and Dion came to pick me up, my mustache was gone and Rick was very pleased.

He told me that I needed a code name for the "House". Rick, my friends and all the people I knew in Philly called me by my nickname, "Pea" which wasn't a catchy name to have in a "House". So I renamed myself "Star D'Amore", I felt that it was catchy and glamorous. The "House of D'Amore" was a big group, and they all loved the new name. Most of them referred to me as "Miss Star". Rick never called me by that name; he continued to call me by my nickname.

I continued to alter my appearance; and it was during this time I began experimenting with makeup. I remember sneaking and using my sister's foundation and mascara. I applied it very lightly so that you really couldn't tell I had it on, and I used clear lip gloss for my lips.

Back then, the girls were wearing those "stick on studs". I adapted this look by putting them on one side of my face and forming them into the shape of a star. I continued to keep my appearance up as well as I could. Manicures, pedicures, arched eyebrows and new outfits became a normal thing. Some of Rick's friends from the "House" began training me on how to "vogue", "walk" and do dance routines.

Kyle and I were always doing exotic designs to jeans. Because we were both creative, we would go to fabric stores and purchase studs, beads and feathers. We always had glue guns and glue sticks to add these things on our clothing. I would wear feathers on my jeans, ripped jeans with studs on them, and different styles of bleached jeans. I was well on my way to becoming a drag queen and didn't even know it. Because there were "rival groups", the "kids" in D'Amore were always practicing, whether we were on 13th Street or at our other hangout spot, at Aaron's house in North Philly.

Rick was the best dancer out of all the people in the group, which made him the Leader. He wanted me to look as good as possible and be able to "vogue" and "walk" and do everything that the group could do, but better. I was never interested in all of that stuff. I just loved being with Rick and looking good. But I loved Rick and I knew how important this was to him. There were times when Rick and some of the boys would come up to my hometown to hang out with me, Dion and Kyle.

Rick met my mother once, but she didn't know he was my "boyfriend". I also met Rick's mother while at his place in North Philly. Our relationship was progressing quickly. Every time Dion, Kyle and I would leave, Rick made me promise to call him to let him know I made it home. I would have to sit on the phone with him until he fell asleep. Rick was the "perfect boyfriend" as long as everything went his way. I knew in my heart that my relationship with Rick wouldn't last, but I had no idea how bad our break-up would be.

The Break Up

As our relationship progressed, things between Rick and I began to get very tense. Rick wanted to become intimate with me but I was not ready for this next phase in our relationship. I kept giving him excuses and pushing him away. He began pressuring me to be intimate with him but I could not. Something in me kept me from going "there" with him. I knew that this would cause tension between the two of us as he began to "ask me for it" in front of our friends. They thought it was "cute" but I didn't. I began to back away from Rick as rumors began surfacing that he was sleeping with other people.

Rick's "true colors" began to show, and he was no longer the loving, attentive, and romantic boyfriend. He turned into a controlling and arrogant monster. Things got so bad between Rick and me that we began to argue (in front of everybody), every time we were in each other's presence.

Rick began to pick fights with me and tell me that I was ugly; he knew that was my weakness. It got to the point that I couldn't stand to even look at him. Our friends got used to our fights, which would end up with me walking away from him, and him following after me. I wanted out of that relationship, and because God had His hand on my life, He gave me a way of escape. I hated Rick and loved him at the same time, but I was no longer "in" love with him. Rick began to drink heavily during this time and this kept me even further away from him which in turn, angered him even more.

The drama in our relationship heightened when Rick began cheating on me with an ex-girlfriend of his, and during this time Dion confessed to me that he slept with Rick when he came to Coatesville. I remember the day Dion told me, and I wasn't even mad. I was so through with Rick that nothing he did or tried to do to me mattered any more. Rick began dating and ex-boyfriend of his who absolutely hated me. I didn't care that they were dating, in fact, I was so happy because I was free.

I knew Rick loved me and that he was trying to hurt me like he felt I had hurt him. The big break up happened on the fourth of July (go figure). During this time I was set on moving on from Rick, but I couldn't escape my history with him as fast as I wanted to. There was a guy that I liked. His name was Brandon. Brandon was in a popular rival "House" crew that was even bigger than D'Amore.

I found out that he felt the same way about me. When we both got the chance to be alone; we talked about the possibility of being together. He said that he knew of my relationship with Rick and (coincidentally), Rick once dated Brandon's ex, who was even more controlling and "crazier" than Rick. We concluded that if we did begin seeing each other, it would cause "havoc" (so to speak). Coincidentally, Brandon was in the same type of situation as I was with Rick. We decided to just be friends.

I was so done with Rick and the drama, and I wanted to move on from him. I stopped going to Philly with Kyle and Dion so that I wouldn't have to deal with Rick. But that didn't stop Rick from calling me. Hanging up on him became a common thing to do. Kyle knew I was completely over Rick so he introduced me to an acquaintance of his. This guy and his friend were supposed to meet us in Philly on 13th Street the night of the fourth of July, but I wasn't sure about going.

Kyle talked me into coming to 13th Street to hang out for the holiday. I had not been to 13th Street for quite some time. So I thought that it would be nice for me to get out and see some of my buddies. I only had one worry, and that was about the possibility of bumping into Rick. When Kyle and I got to 13th Street, it was packed and my buddies were very glad to see me. We sat on one of the stoops and laughed and had a good time. "Brandon" came over and hugged me and we had light conversation. I was happy to see him. Brandon left just in time because shortly afterwards, a "drunken" Rick came strolling around the corner and my heart stopped. We all knew that something was going to "pop off". He spotted me and made his way over to me. I wanted to leave, but I knew that I had to face him. Rick spoke to me and remained as cordial as he could. He then proceeded to give me a big sloppy kiss. I pushed him away and walked off with Rick on my heels. Kyle, Dion (who was there with Aaron), and some others stood close by.

I walked toward the alley that held a Lesbian club. I politely asked Rick to leave me alone and I told him that we were over. He began telling me that he loved me, and he actually became a little emotional. But I was done with him. When he saw that I would not change my decision, he became angry. We had words with each other that got louder and louder, until Rick got so angry that he tried to attack me. Just at that moment, my friends came around the corner to hold Rick back, and Kyle and some acquaintances of mine pulled up in front of us.

A buddy of mine happened to be a very tall "butch" lesbian who dared Rick to touch me again (she was one of the ones the confronted Marlon earlier that year). She and Kyle put me in the car with some other girls and we drove off. I remember crying in the car with Kyle doing his best to console me. I knew that the breakup was final. After they drove me around for awhile, they took us back to get Kyle's car and Kyle drove me home.

Moving On

After the big breakup with Rick, I stayed home for the rest of the summer. Kyle and Dion still had their boyfriends, and stayed in the city as much as they could. The acquaintance that I had met through Kyle apologized for not showing up (I was relieved that he didn't). I told him what happened between Rick and I that night. He and I became friends and kept in touch that summer. But nothing became of our "friendship".

Dion would come and visit me; sometimes bringing with him some of my buddies from our "D'Amore" clique. Kyle had decided to move to Philly with some friends of ours, so I didn't see much of him, but he called all the time. Rick still tried to call and check on me but he knew we were over. I had left the whole Rick and "Star D'Amore" thing behind.

By the time September came, I found myself in a new relationship with someone I met earlier that year in Philly, when Kyle and I first started to venture to the city. His name was Darren. Darren became my third and final relationship. During that time I had become close friends with a guy who happened to grow up with my sisters. In my hometown, everyone knows everyone. The older male's name was "Shawn". Shawn was considered a Legend of the gay community in my hometown and very well respected. I felt very safe around him because he knew my family very well.

A couple of years prior to me becoming friends with Shawn, he actually protected me from a man who literally wanted to "kill" me because I had a "crush" on him. Of course I thought that I had real friends that I could share that with, but unfortunately in my hometown, gossip spreads like a wildfire. This particular man was furious and he came out looking for me. Shawn happened to stop the man in his tracks and talked him out of beating me up. Like I said in a previous chapter, in my mind, I was a girl. Reality was hidden from me when I saw a boy that I wanted. The devil really had my mind, but today I thank God for His delivering power.

Now back to Darren; I met him in a "speakeasy" late one night in Philly, when Kyle and I first started frequenting the city earlier that year. For those of you who don't know what a "speakeasy" is, it is what you would call a "hole in the wall". Most of the places are located in cellars. This particular place was in someone's cellar, which had been turned into a bar. Darren and I held a light conversation that night and I had not seen him since.

Following my breakup with Rick, I stayed home, and became a "hermit", so to speak. One particular evening, Kyle called me and said that someone wanted to meet me. It was

Darren, we began to talk everyday on the phone. Shortly afterwards we began dating, and Darren was very affectionate. He was the perfect guy, too perfect. I told Darren about my past failed relationships. He knew Marlon very well because the two of them went to school together, and he also new Rick by acquaintance. I felt that Darren was rushing me into a serious relationship way too fast. Darren planned a day for me to come down to Philly to see him. He had his best friend from a nearby city come pick me up.

This particular friend of Darren's happened to be an "Elder" in a church. He was also married, with two children. You would have never known he was a "closeted homosexual". This is what you would call a "down low brother". Down low brothers are very manly men who secretly struggles with homosexual desires. Some of these men are Pastors, leaders, husbands and fathers. "Dow low" men don't believe they are gay, and they despise very feminine men. The spirit of homosexuality is a very strong spirit that has enslaved the minds of many men all over the world; but I will address this issue at another time. Darren's friend came to pick me up and we rode down to the city, and to Darren's house.

On this particular date with Darren, we ended up on 13th Street. When we got there I had mixed emotions. I was no longer "Miss Star D'Amore" with all the fabulousness; I was just Louis again and I was dressed very plainly. I didn't want anyone to recognize me and I didn't want to bring attention to myself. When we got there I saw many new faces, which made me feel a little more comfortable. I had all black on and I wore a very long black scarf. Darren said that I looked like his "little woman". I didn't want to run into anybody I knew, especially Rick. I clung onto Darren as much as I could. Then the thing that I dreaded the most happened, I saw Rick.

Darren told me prior to us coming to 13th Street that he didn't want me to worry about Rick because he was with me. Rick didn't speak to me and I was so relieved. By this time, I was ready to leave, as we were leaving, we ran smack dab into Marlon, who needed Darren to drop him off somewhere. He was glad to see me and began flirting with me until Darren put an immediate stop to that. Marlon said "Oh that's you Darren?" "My bad". Darren and I got to spend a little alone time together, but I knew that I didn't want to be in a relationship right now.

By the time I got home, I knew that I had to end it with Darren. He wanted to move way too fast and I wasn't ready. I told my friend "Shawn" about Darren, and Shawn wanted to meet him. Darren and his best friend come up to Coatesville and hung out with Shawn and I. By this time, Darren's friend and I became good friends and kept in touch often. Shawn and Darren's friend got along great and enjoyed a good conversation.

I had to deal with Darren being overly affectionate, and I couldn't stand it any longer. He was the "man" in our relationship, but he was very needy. He even began planning long term things for our relationship. The more Darren pushed and pushed for our relationship to move faster, the more he pushed me further away from him. When Darren and his friend left I knew that I was definitely ready to end the relationship.

I felt like Darren was suffocating me and I ended our relationship over the phone, which didn't go too well. During this time in my life, I didn't want the bother of a relationship because it seemed to be too much for me. For the remainder of that year, I did not return to the city. My mother helped me to get a job where she was working and I focused on that. I had been out of work just about that whole year and I was grateful to find a full time job, where I remained for four years.

CHAPTER 5

Party Animal

For the wages of sin is death...Romans 6:23 KJV

I will never forget the year I turned 21. I was set on partying and having fun. I had new friends that were all women, and we hung out around town and hit the bar scene very hard. I remember the time Shawn came to get me to celebrate my 21st birthday. We both stood outside of a well known bar in Coatesville, and waited until the clock struck twelve a.m. As soon as the clock struck, I pranced inside of that bar and the rest was history.

I had a ball with my friends; I had so many people calling my cell phone that I remember coming home from work and turning my phone off just to get some rest. We even hung out at the bars during the week. There was one particular bar in Coatesville that was my favorite bar. We would sit in that particular bar for hours drinking long island ice teas, and playing music on the juke box. I loved all my "girlfriends" dearly, but I began to miss the attention of a man.

There were guys that I had met from Philly, who I continued

to talk to, but it didn't fill the void on the inside of me. I had not been in a relationship since "Darren", and I had no desire to be in a real relationship. I just wanted to have fun and meet new men.

The previous year, I had lost a lot of weight from me running the streets and going through with "Rick". By this time, I had gained that weight back, as well as my confidence.

I came out in "full force"- tight ripped jeans, sheer tops, tank tops, bandanas tied around my head (that was "in" back then), and other exotic clothing. By now, I began carrying designer "clutches" (female pocketbooks without the handle). All of those things were natural to me in my mind. I began wearing makeup again. I applied liquid foundation very light on my face; and I wore fake "hazel colored" contacts, mascara and lip gloss. I loved the way I looked and I was now ready to hit the gay bar scene again.

Return to 13th Street

It was exciting to be able to freely hit the bar scene on 13th Street. For the longest time we used to hang out outside of the clubs, but now I was old enough to go in. However, the most fun was still just walking around 13th Street. I remember how the men would pull over in their cars to try to talk to me. This time, my friend "Shawn" was with me and he always got a lot of attention when we went to 13th Street together. Sometimes Kyle came along with us.

One particular evening, Shawn Kyle and I went to 13th Street, and I ran into "Rick". We remained cordial with each other. We held a light conversation with each other and that was it. "Rick" looked great, but I didn't let that deter me. I felt that Rick and I were much better at being friends than we were as a couple. My focus was meeting new men with "no strings attached".

With this newfound confidence I had, I became much bolder in my approach to men. I was no longer the "coy" one who shied away from men. If I saw someone I wanted I went after them. Such was the case with "Alton". On night Shawn, a friend of ours, and I drove down to 13th Street just to hang out and get a drink. We had fun as usual just "shooting the breeze". As we were getting ready to leave I was standing outside waiting for Shawn to meet me around the corner. This guy drove by me very slow and locked eyes with me.

I gave him a look as well which prompted him to drive around again. When he passed me he stared again. I knew by then he wanted to talk to me. But at that time we were getting ready to leave so I didn't think I would see him again. As

Shawn began driving I noticed that "Alton" was in front of us. I told Shawn to stop that car. Shawn flagged him down and got him to pull over. Shawn parked behind him and I got out of the car and sauntered over to him. This time I became the "hunter" and I played the role well. It left him speechless. We exchanged telephone numbers and I got back in Shawn's car and we went home laughing about what I did.

The next day I spoke to "Alton". He said he wanted to come up and see me. I gave him the address and he typed it in and got the directions. I would see him once I got off of work. I got home and freshened up and by the time I was done, he had pulled up in front of my house. He was somewhat "preppy" which was very different from the men I've dated.

I introduced him to my sister and then we headed out for a drive. We then stopped at a friend of mine's house to hang out there for a while. Although I had a nice time, it was something about him that I couldn't get with. I decided not to continue communication with him. I continued to enjoy going to the gay bars and hanging out with friends.

There was a particular gay bar-club on 13th Street that I always went to. Though I enjoyed the bar-club scene, the "action" was found outside. I found fulfillment in the attention that men gave me. I loved being able to flirt with men freely.

But even though I was having the time of my life, I knew deep down inside that my days were numbered. I knew that the Lord was not pleased with my lifestyle. I didn't have a "miserable life of sin", in fact when the Lord gave me my final ultimatum, I came back to the Lord "kicking and screaming". But there were days that my mind was in turmoil over the fact that I knew I had to give this all up soon, but the reality was that I didn't want to.

On the outside, you wouldn't have known that I was in turmoil. I was a young man called of God to preach the Gospel and set the captive free. Yet, here I was at 21 years old with makeup on, tight ripped jeans, and a pocketbook; looking for the love of a man out in the streets of Philadelphia at night. I remember one time in particular, when a man had me in an alley on 13th Street, "hemmed up" against the wall. He was feeling on me and doing different things, I looked up in the sky and remembered the prophecy that said "The eyes of God are watching you and following you wherever you go".

Me and My "Girls"

The majority of my life has been spent with hanging out with girls. I have learned many things just by being around women all of my life. Girls accepted me, and they made me feel like I was one of them. My "girls" never made me feel like I was a disgrace. They accepted me and I loved them for it. For many years, in my interactions with women, they would slip and say to me "gggiiiirrrrrlllll. I was skilled at communication with a woman as if I was a woman; that's why I understood why they slipped up.

When we all went out to party, I was the "faggot" among the bunch. I watched how men gave them attention and flirted with them. It reminded me of the attention I received when I went to gay bars and clubs. In my mind, I wanted to be like them but I knew that would never happen. Partying with the girls became a "full time job". I would come home from work, rest and then meet some of my "girlfriends" at a particular bar and we would stay there until closing. There were times when I came home drunk early in the morning, only to have to get up an hour and a half later to go to work.

By now, I was very comfortable with who I was. I was "the life of the party", when I was in the presence of my friends. I knew how to entertain my friends and keep them laughing all the time. I was always thinking of ways to draw attention to myself. One thing I remember doing is ordering a drink called "snake bite"- this was liquor that you had to light with a match and drink it down with a straw while it was on fire. I used that to gain attention from the men in the bar. My girlfriends would cheer me on as I sucked that drink down. It caused everybody that was around to focus their attention on me.

I was also a dancer. If my "song" came on while being at a bar and club, I would scream very loud and then grab one of my friends and dance all night. At a gay bar I was totally different. I would dance like a girl. I would twirl my hips and "back it up" all the things I've seen my "girlfriends" do. I partied very hard, but as I got a little older, I calmed down a lot.

By then I began hanging out with my female cousins. This was a slightly older crowd, but that didn't bother me at all. I had some of the times of my life hanging with them. Being with my cousins felt safe to me and I didn't have to worry about anybody trying to "clown" me or disrespect me. We would hang out at my cousin's house and drink and laugh all night long. There were times when we went out, but mostly we hung out at my cousin's house. Even in all the fun I was having with them, I still had a "void" that only a man could fill.

A "Down Low" Affair

The men that I dated were men that were straight appearing, but hung out in the gay community. This one particular man I met caused me to really see the reality of "down low brothers".

There was an older gay couple that I knew, who were close to me. One of the men had a brother that lived in another state but came to visit. This couple lived in Philly and was hosting a small "get together" at their home.

I bought a girlfriend down with me, we both met the brother that was visiting. He was very tall, dark skinned and bald headed. He was very polite but he seemed like he was the quiet one out of the bunch. It wasn't until my friend and I were saying goodbye to this man named "Mike" that I noticed he began flirting with me. When I shook his hand, he held on longer than usual and the way he looked at me caused me to wonder. My suspicions were not confirmed until the next day when I sent a text message to Mike's brother telling him that Mike was cute.

Later that night, I was hanging out at the home of a friend of mine, when I received a text message from a telephone number that I didn't recognize. The message was telling me how sexy I was. I immediately knew who it was and from there, we texted each other all night long. I felt those "butterflies" that you feel when you first meet someone. I knew that Mike was only in the city for a few weeks, but it didn't matter to me. I began to "catch feelings" for Mike quickly.

In getting to know him, I found out that he was in his mid-thirties and that he had two children and he was on the brink of divorce. None of that bothered me because I was excited to be dating a "real" man. We began to make plans with each other for the duration of his visit. I know that it was stupid to fall in love with a man you just met, and especially a closeted homosexual man with so much baggage.

The Lord intervened and cause Mike's trip to be cut very short. When he told me one night that he had to leave the very next day, it felt as if my heart dropped. Mike wanted to see me before he left. I immediately dragged one of my girlfriends down to the city with me to go see him. When we got there, Mike's brother hosted a small cookout for him. I left my friend outside to mingle while I went looking for Mike. He was upstairs near his bedroom talking quietly on the phone.

I knew something was up because everyone else was outside in the backyard and he was in that huge house upstairs on the phone. I sat on his bed and waited for him to come out and greet me. He finally came and greeted me but it was very nonchalant. He was totally different from the man I was conversing with over the phone for the past few days.

He wanted to go outside where everyone else was. I introduced him to my friend and he flirted with her the whole night. I felt stupid for falling for this man. My friend was ready to leave early, and she was very upset. I asked her what was wrong, and she said that she would tell me in the car. My friend immediately went to her car and waited out front for me. Mike walked me out front to the car and we said our goodbyes. He hugged me and waited until I was in the car, and then he left. As we were leaving, my friend began to tell me how Mike was "hitting" on her behind my back. She said that when she asked him about me, he said that I didn't mean anything to him. I couldn't believe just how sneaky this man was. His brother later told me that Mike was "messing" with another woman while he was staying there.

For weeks after he went back home, I went through the process of getting over him. During this time we would email each other and he would send me a text message often. I found out that Mike was in a lot of trouble in his area, which caused his trip to be cut very short. It wasn't until weeks later I finally began moving on from Mike. The "last straw" for me is when he finally called my cell phone. I looked at the phone and for some reason I couldn't answer the phone. He left a message stating that he needed me to "wire" him some money ASAP. I responded to him via email telling him goodbye for good. I deleted his phone number and removed his email address and moved on.

Reconnecting with the Past

Later that year, Gay Pride weekend was happening in the city on 13th Street. I drove down with another homosexual male friend of mine. I saw some old buddies of mine and shortly afterwards I ran into "Marlon". We were very happy to see each other. We exchanged phone numbers and we promised to keep in touch.

I was eager to reconnect with him and couldn't wait to talk to him again. Later on that night, my friend and I were sitting on a stoop when "Rick" and some guys walked past. When Rick saw me he hugged and we talked a little. I was genuinely happy to see him. I had gotten over our past as a couple and was ready to be just a friend to him.

After that night, I began talking to Marlon. We began a long distance relationship. This time I was very careful not to get too attached to him. I knew he was a "player", but I really liked him and thought that this time around he would be different. Things between us were going good for a while but then he started becoming "distant". During this time "Rick" and I would talk over the phone periodically.

We were becoming good friends. When we first got together, we never gave each other the time to develop a friendship, so this was very new to us. Shortly afterwards I let

Marlon go for good. I knew he didn't want a long distance relationship, and every time I planned to go see him, something would prevent me from going.

"Rick" knew whom I was dating because we would both talk about the relationships we were in at the time. But after my break up, I began to regain feelings for "Rick again. He was older, more mature and more "laid back", so to speak. Rick and I took things very slow this time. I knew that after three years, he still had feelings for me.

By the time December of that year came, I was ready to become "intimate" with him. We both planned a weekend for him to come up. But mysteriously, after we made those plans, I changed my mind. I could not go through with it, and I cut off communication with him. I have learned that God is an awesome protector. But the thing is, it was never about me! He had to protect His word concerning my life. There were many things that I could have gotten into, but God has prevented it. He foresaw what He has ordained me to become, and has preserved me for such a time as this.

I moved on both from Marlon and Rick for the final time. At this time, I ceased from returning to 13th Street to hang out. Because I partied so hard between the ages of 21-22, by the time I turned 23 I was tired of the party scene. I calmed down a whole lot. By now I was comfortable in who I was as a homosexual young man. By this time I wore acrylic on my nails and my hair was permed straight. I did different styles with it and I wore it in an auburn color.

I was so messed up in my mind. But I wasn't ready to give it all up. I was content with my life and friends. I occasionally went to have a drink with my friends but most of my hanging out was down at my cousin's house where me and the girls hung out and laughed and drank all night long. To me that was the life. I had no complaints. But I didn't know the great pain that the year 2004 would have in store for me. My life was about to change in the most drastic way.

<u>To the Reader</u>

Dear Reader, you have read my story from my birth up until my young adulthood. You have journeyed with me through my former lifestyle. I truly believe that the deeper you go in your testimony the more the enemy is exposed for who he really is. This causes true deliverance for the ones who have struggled with the same things I have.

It was hard reliving my past, but as long as one person is touched, that's worth it all. As detailed as this portion of my testimony was, there were many things that I left out. I dug as deep as God allowed for me to tell my story.

You have read how the enemy has tried to take my life. You read about the perversion, my failed relationships, and my past failures. In my next book you will read how God used devastation to get my attention once and for all. The second half of this journey deals with my transition from a homosexual wandering the streets of a gay populated section of Philadelphia, looking for the love of a man, to a man of God seeking his true identity.

You will read about the severe "church hurt" that I had to endure, and the series of betrayals that I experienced. You will journey with me from my season of testing and trial, to my severe struggle with the spirit of poverty and lack. But most importantly, you will witness as God carried me and covered me through it all. If it had not been for the Lord, I wouldn't be here to even write this book. He promised never to leave nor forsake me, and He has truly kept His word.

In conclusion, as in Romans 8:28: ***"And we know that all things work together for good to them that love God, and are called according to His purpose."***

ABOUT THE AUTHOR

Louis Trammell was born and raised in Coatesville, Pennsylvania. Well known for his artistic and creative abilities he is a talented artist and designer.

Louis is a dynamic Preacher of the Gospel having received his Minister's License under the Leadership of Bishop Greg M. Davis and Pastor Kim A. Davis. He is a sought after prayer warrior and spiritual warfare strategist

Louis is presently a member of Greater Deliverance International where the Senior Pastor is Apostle Bobby G. Duncan.

Louis is now a celebrated Author having told his awesome testimony in his first of three books: Destined To Do Damage. This is an account of Louis plunge into the world of Homosexuality.

It is his prayer that he is able to reach out to those who struggle with being free from Homosexuality, Lesbianism and the "Down Low" syndrome.

He received a recent prophesy that He is called to reach those that the Church is afraid to reach.

This is one facet of his Ministry and His greatest desire is to please the Lord. May you be blessed by the Ministry of Louis Trammell.

www.ingramcontent.com/pod-product-compliance
Lightning Source LLC
Chambersburg PA
CBHW031259290426
44109CB00012B/648